# LOOK INSIDE
# FRANCE

Ian James
&
Joy Richardson

Photography by Chris Fairclough

Watts Books

London ● New York ● Sydney

# CONTENTS

©1995 Watts Books
96 Leonard Street
London EC2A 4RH

Franklin Watts Australia
14 Mars Road
Lane Cove
NSW 2066

A differentiated text edition
of **Inside France** first published in
1988.

Design: Edward Kinsey
Cover design: Nina Kingsbury
Illustrations: Hayward Art Group

UK ISBN: 0 7496 1877 9

Printed in Belgium

A CIP catalogue record for this
book is available from the Britsh
Library.

Dewey Decimal Classification:
914.6

**Additional photographs:**

Mansell Collection 8; Popperfoto 9;
Kobal Collection: 22 (b); Phillips
Collection 22 (t)
Front cover: ZEFA
Frontispiece: Chris Fairclough

# The land

## France is one of the largest countries in Europe.

It is bigger than Spain, bigger than Germany, twice as big as Britain but smaller than Russia and Ukraine.

France has sea on two sides and touches seven other countries.

The highest mountain is Mont Blanc in the Alps near Italy. There is always snow on top of Mont Blanc.

**Below:** Brittany is in the north of France.

**Left:** People can ski in the snowy Alps.

**Below:** The River Seine runs through Paris, the capital city.

**Above:** The French Riviera by the Mediterranean Sea is popular for holidays.

# The longest river in France is the River Loire.

It flows over 1000km across France to the west coast. The River Seine flows out into the English Channel in the north. The River Rhône flows south into the Mediterranean Sea.

The south of France is hot and dry.
The north is cooler and wetter.

# The people and their history

## France has seen lots of changes during its long history.

Celtic peoples settled there before the Romans arrived.

Then German tribes invaded, including the Franks who gave France its name.

Hundreds of years later, strong kings made the whole of France into one country.

**Below:** Louis XIV ruled for 77 years. He made France very powerful.

**Above:** The guillotine was used to cut off people's heads during the French Revolution.

# In 1789 there was a revolution in France.

The people defeated the King. Napoleon then set out to conquer most of Europe for France.

In the first and second world wars, France was overrun by Germany.

France is now a peaceful country. It is a republic and people vote to choose the President.

**Above:** Napoleon (on the white horse) was defeated at the Battle of Waterloo in 1815.

**Left:** General Charles de Gaulle claiming Paris back from the Germans in 1944. He became President of France.

9

# Towns and cities

## 57 million people live in France.

There is twice as much space per person as there is in Britain. It is one of the least crowded countries in Europe.

Most people used to live in the countryside, working on small farms. Now machinery has taken over. Today four out of five people live in towns and cities.

**Below:** A country area in southeastern France.

**Right:** The city of Lille is in the middle of a big industrial area.

**Below:** Many villages like Dinan in Brittany have looked much the same for hundreds of years.

**Above:** Marseille, the ancient port in southeastern France.

# Paris is the capital city of France.

Nine million people live there. The five biggest cities in France are Paris, Lyon, Marseille, Lille and Bordeaux. Marseille is the main port for ships.

Many towns and cities still have old buildings in the middle. New houses, offices and factories have grown up around them.

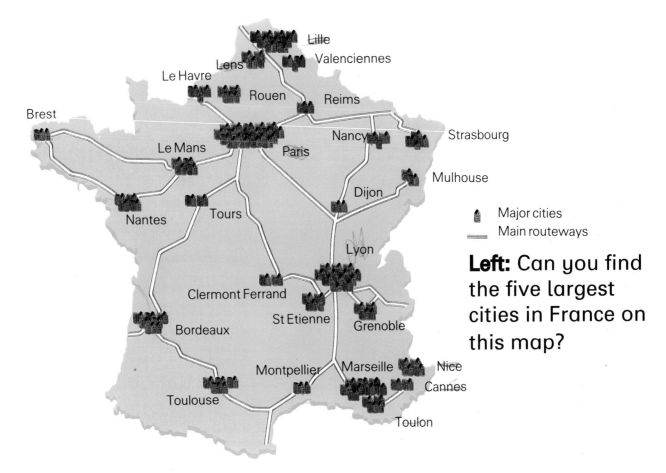

Le Havre · Lens · Lille · Valenciennes · Rouen · Reims · Brest · Le Mans · Paris · Nancy · Strasbourg · Mulhouse · Nantes · Tours · Dijon · Clermont Ferrand · Lyon · St Etienne · Grenoble · Bordeaux · Montpellier · Marseille · Nice · Cannes · Toulouse · Toulon

Major cities
Main routeways

**Left:** Can you find the five largest cities in France on this map?

**Left:** In this view of Paris can you see some old buildings and some new buildings? The Eiffel Tower is in the distance.

# Paris is a very beautiful city.

To begin with, Paris was just a little island in the River Seine. Since then it has grown much bigger.

Now there are lots of fine buildings. The Louvre, an old royal palace, is one of the world's largest museums. The Eiffel Tower reaches up into the sky. You can see all over the city from the top.

**Below:** Can you find these buildings on the plan of Paris?

1 Chaillot Palace
2 Eiffel Tower
3 Arc de Triomphe
4 Invalides
5 Place de la Concorde
6 Opera
7 The Louvre
8 Sacré-Coeur
9 The Bourse
10 Luxembourg Palace
11 Pantheon
12 Notre Dame

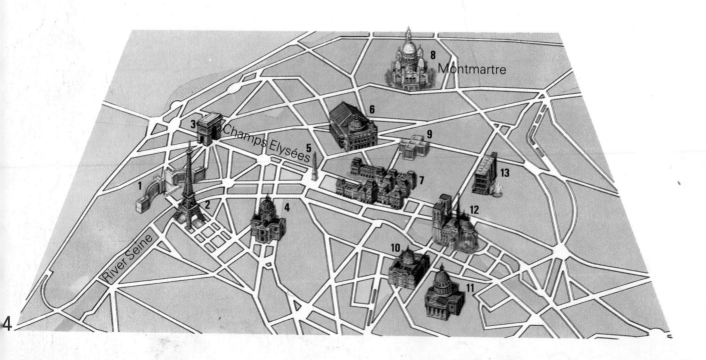

# Family life

## Families like to spend lots of time together.

Mealtimes are special occasions for enjoying good food and sharing all the news.

Families live in houses or apartments. Most homes are modern, though some old country houses still do not have electricity.

**Below:** A French family outside their home.

**Left:** Many families live in a modern apartment which they rent or buy.

**Below:** Lots of people grow vegetables in their garden.

# Food

## The French are famous for their cooking.

People buy fresh bread, meat, fruit and vegetables in markets and little shops as well as in supermarkets.

Breakfast is usually coffee or chocolate with bread or pastries. Lunch is the main meal.

Snails are eaten as a special treat. French wines are usually excellent.

**Below:** Stalls selling vegetables and cooked meats.

**Above:** Adults often drink wine with their meals.

**Left:** The French like food to look good as well as taste good.

18

# Sports and pastimes

## Cycling and soccer are popular.

The Tour de France is a world-famous cycle race around France.

In parks, people play boules, a game of bowls with metal balls.

Most people have a holiday in August. Some families  go camping. Many people enjoy ski-ing in winter.

**Below:** Cycling is a popular sport and good exercise.

**Above:** A seaside holiday resort on the west coast of France.

**Left:** People play boules on any piece of flat ground.

# The arts

## France is famous for a lot of great architecture, painting, writing and music.

There are many ancient cathedrals with stained glass windows and spires pointing to the sky.

Painters like Monet and Renoir lived in France and made great paintings from the sights around them. People around the world now enjoy their paintings in art galleries.

**Below:** This cathedral is in Amiens, by the River Somme.

**Above:** Auguste Renoir painted *The Luncheon of the Boating Party* one hundred years ago in France.

**Left:** Long ago, Victor Hugo wrote *The Hunchback of Notre Dame* which was made into a film.

# Farming

## France makes a lot of its money from farming.

Four-fifths of the land is used for growing crops and feeding animals.

In many parts of the country, rich soil produces good grass which feeds the cows to make meat and milk. Some of the milk is used to make famous French cheeses. Grapes for wine grow on vines.

**Below:** In some parts of France, tractors have not yet taken over from animals.

**Above:** Vines growing in a sunny vineyard.

**Left:** A choice of cheeses at a market stall.

# Industry

## Lots of things are made in France.

One person in five works in industry, making goods to sell at home and to export to other countries.

Mining provides the metal to make machinery. Factories produce cars and chemicals.

France grows enough food for itself and sells some to other countries. The money from exports pays for the imports France wants.

**Below:** Many modern cars are French.

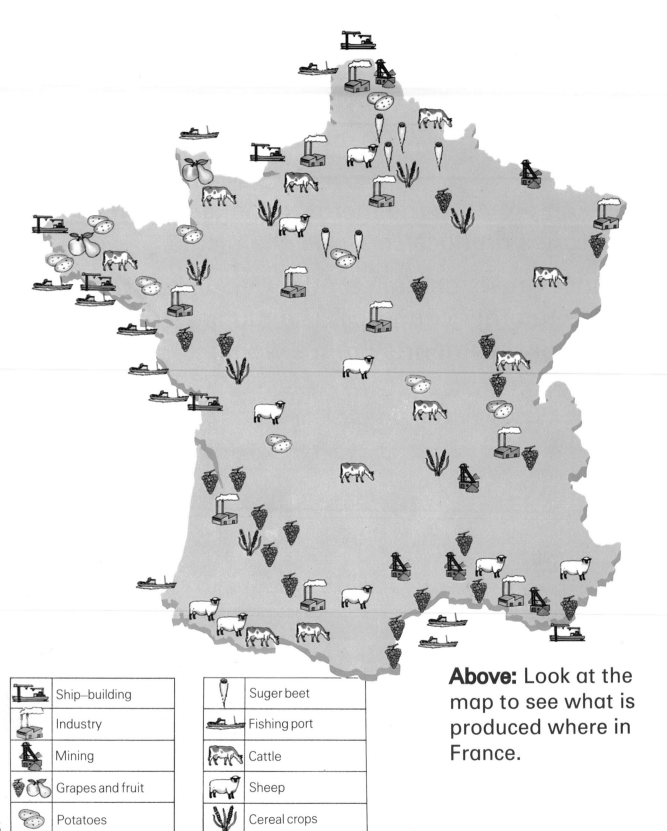

| | | | | |
|---|---|---|---|---|
| | Ship–building | | Suger beet |
| | Industry | | Fishing port |
| | Mining | | Cattle |
| | Grapes and fruit | | Sheep |
| | Potatoes | | Cereal crops |

**Above:** Look at the map to see what is produced where in France.

26

**Left:** France leads the world in fashion design.

# France sells wine to other countries.

It also exports perfumes and fashion clothes from top designers.

France does not have enough coal and oil of its own so it has to import some from abroad.

France makes its own electricity. Some power stations use water power to save on fuel.

# Looking to the future

## France has changed since World War II and is still changing.

Lots of people died in the war. Many buildings were bombed and most factories were destroyed.

After the war, France had to work hard to become a rich industrial country.

**Below:** The parents of many French children came from countries which used to be ruled by France.

**Above:** This modern furnace is heated by the sun through solar panels.

# France is using scientific inventions and new technology to keep its industry up to date.

The French language is still a main world language.

France is a member of the European Union. It wants to be a strong country in a successful Europe. It is looking to the future.

# Facts about France

**Area:**
547,026 sq km

**Population:**
57,690,000

**Capital:**
Paris

**Largest Cities:**
(Populations include cities and suburbs)
Paris (9,060,000)
Lyon (1,262,000)
Marseille (1,087,000)
Lille (950,000)
Bordeaux (685,000)

**Official language:**
French

**Religion:**
Christianity

**Main exports:**
Machinery and transportation equipment, chemicals, food and farm products

**Unit of currency:**
Franc

## France compared with other countries

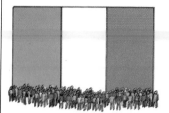

**France** 105 per sq km

**Britain** 238 per sq km

**Australia** 2 per sq km

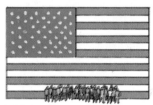

**USA** 27 per sq km

**Above:** How many people? France is less heavily populated than most European countries.

**Below:** How large? France is large in European terms but much smaller than the United States or Australia.

USA          Australia          France   UK

**Below:** Some French money and stamps. One franc is divided into 100 centimes.

30

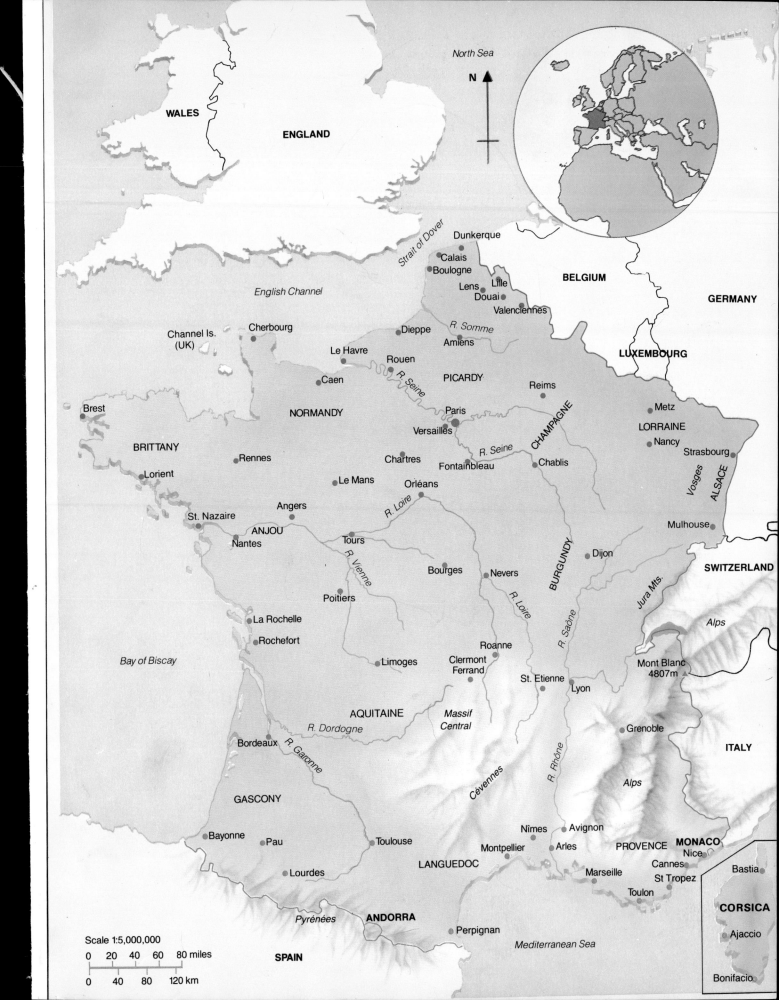

# Index